Copyright © 2018 Chris Gibbs

First Edition

ISBN 978-1-9996363-0-2

Published by Inner Version Ltd
www.innerversion.com

I — PERSONAL PHILOSOPHY

I. Any personal philosophy
    Should be adapted to the individual,
    Selecting the concepts that resonate
    The most deeply.

II. Philosophical values
    Should be attributes
    Attainable by all.

III. No philosophical system
    Should be thought of as complete;
    Ideas from other sources
    Always should be sought.

IV. The unique blend
    Of different philosophies
    Promotes variety and vibrancy.

II — PONDER THE BEFORE

I. The slowest to attain
    Wisdom wins the race.

II. Reflections take time
    Echoing words
    With hidden depths.

III — ONE POINT

I. The tempting tree of a thousand
    Branches – each tip
    Blossoms once.

II. Early wandering of attention
    Can be subtle
Until the growing mist
    Obscures the view.

III. Gathering to a single point of focus
    Increases strength,
    Improves enjoyment.

IV — BECOMING LUCID

I.   Recording dreams through stillness
        After waking is the first
        Step towards lucidity.

II.   Upon encountering a common dream
        Scenario, the self poses
        The question of reality . . . .

III.   . . . . One subconscious exploit
        Is the pressing of one finger
            Into the other palm: a moment
        Of dream exhilaration transpires
            When it goes straight through.

IV.   As conscious verifying of reality
        Habitually filters into dream behaviour
        Behaviour, lucidity increases.

V — SUSTAINING LUCIDITY

I.   Initial forays into lucid dreaming
    Present a challenge
    In containing the excitement.

II. Repeating at short intervals
Reality verification
    Can sustain the extraordinary
    Experience of a lucid dream.

VI — THE DREAM WORLD

I. Some dreams reveal
   Your true inner version, unhindered
   By the insecurities and peculiarities
   Of the conscious mind.

II. Only in the dream world
    Do external reasons fully
    Justify an action.

III. My life's purpose:
     To experience fully the present
     Moment, pausing momentarily
     To fantasise overnight.

VII — THE SUBCONSCIOUS

I. The subconscious mind is nature's finest
    Instrument, honed and tuned
      To realise visions as received consciously.

II. Most great ideas arrive spontaneously
      During periods of idle mind —
    Periods with a direct open channel
      From the subconscious to the surface.

III. Planning a time for spontaneity
      Is paradoxical;
    Preparing the mind for a time
      Is achievable.

IV. An empty presence
      Sharpens focus,
        Refills the subconscious.

VIII — TWO STREAMS ALIGNED

I. Being slow in practice
   Draws first the best ideas.

II. Taking pause in action
    Allows the deeper stream to realign.

IX — BREAKING PATTERNS

I. True inspiration arises
   Out of sources unexpected.

II. Only in testing patterns unverified
   Can truth be generalised.

III. Detachment holds
   No breakable cycle.

X — THE DELETE RULE

I. Superfluous parts removed,
    Artistic power increases.

XI — GROUNDED CREATION

I. Dispelling notions about future admiration
    Brings more attention to the work.

II. The world does not wait
    For your creation.

XII — THE WORK DIVERSE

I. The obsolete potential of most
     Work provides good practice
     In detachment from results.

II. Compassion gracefully
        Descends into the process,
    Detachment naturally
        Arises from the outcome.

III. Impermanence creates
        The diverse surface.

XIII — SWIRLS IN THE DUST

I.   Mountains of sand
        Appear impressive
        From an ant's eye view.

II.   Mighty dunes
        Upon realising their might
        Surrender to the wind.

III.   Each imprint in the dust
        Uniquely sets the scene
        For future patterns.

XIV — THE DISCONNECT

I. The person and the name —
   Connected for convenience only.

II. The person and the role —
   Detached for effortless results.

III. The person and the list of tasks —
   Linked freely to enjoy the flow.

IV. The person and the train of thought —
   Same driver, different destination.

XV — ALMOST DESIRE

I. The overlap with future desire
    Appears as a shadow past.

II. Almost all there is to achieve
    Is achieved already.

III. Almost-desire is practised,
    Required effort reduces.

XVI — PRESENT GREATNESS

I.   Greatness need not be assigned
        Exclusively to history.

II.   Continuing greatness
        Is greatness itself.

XVII — LOSS IN CONTROL

I. One portion of control
    Is lost to every moment.

II. The limits of control, now recognised —
    Relaxes the sphere,
    Dissolves the boundary.

XVIII — MODEST WISDOM

I. Self-promotion of temporal
   Highs in circumstances
Points to insecurity.

II. Inner beauty refrains
    From advertising its beauty.

III. Taking the credit
     Creates resentment;
Giving credit away
     Creates encouragement.

IV. Selfish comparison
    Increases insecurity;
Unselfish comparison
    Increases wisdom.

XIX — MUTUAL REFLECTION

I.   The mirror above
        Blames and reflects condescension;
    The mirror below
        Praises and reflects constructive thought.

II.   Interest gives
        And reflects interest;
    Passion gives
        And reflects passion;
    Completeness gives —
        And reflects completely.

XX — ENERGY FLOW

I. Cool inner, cool outer:
   Thinks and invites correctness.

II. Warm inner, cool outer:
   Feels and invites acceptance.

III. Warm inner, warm outer:
   Displays and welcomes engagement.

IV. Cool inner, warm outer:
   Reveals and welcomes conciseness.

XXI — OPEN TO THE WILD

I. Densely crowded
Space reduces
Friendliness of
Chance encounters.

II. Natural communication opens
    With each step
        Towards the wild.

XXII — COMBINED RESET

I.   Judgement suspends
        Akin to the way normally
        Reserved for flawless idols.

II.   Admiration restores
        For all the positive
        Qualities in every being.

XXIII — ADVICE TWO WAYS

I. Advice released carefree
   Returns without requirement.

II. The best advice invites
   A longer time to process.

XXIV — LIFE UNRATED

I. Rating events in progress
   Detracts from life enjoyment.

II. Life begins
   With minimal preconception;
Experience completes
   With only essential announcement.

XXV — HYPERBOLE AND OVER-HYPE

I. Hyperbole assumes
   As standard truth unquestioned,
Yet originating often
   In a notion of the time.

II. Over-hype inflates
   Opinions only single
To form an aggravated view
   On future actions and events.

III. Hyperbole and over-hype:
   Increasing one
   Tends to increase the other.

XXVI — SIMPLE BEING

I. The male wood pigeon perched
         Upon the lamppost,
    Oblivious to the reason for the traffic
         Steaming through his territory —
    And yet he finds fulfilment
         In his local world.

II. The ambling mind
         In regular routine
    Appreciates the simple
         With experience anew.

XXVII — FIELD ALIGNMENT

I. From every seat of consciousness
    Extends a line
    Through the space eternal.

II. When knots are straightened
    Flows true expression.

III. Moving across the field
    Generates excitement.

XXVIII — DAILY CONTRAST

I. Full black and white
   Lurk in grey noise.

II. Infinite falls and rises
    Lie in waves unmagnified.

XXIX — SURFACE WAVES

I.   Having no fixed
        Opinions to defend,
    The sandcastle yields
        To the incoming tide.

II.   Filling and emptying
        With no preferred state,
    The rock pool accepts
        The recurring waves.

III.   Established firmly
        On deep and steady ground,
    The harbour wall offers welcome relief
        Against the buffeting sea.

IV.   Your inner version dwells
        In the slow depths of the ocean,
    Unchanged by ripples
        At the surface.

XXX — CHALLENGE THE DEEP

I. Doubt tends to resurface
    Shortly after being submerged.

II. A vessel of uncertainty
    Can be used to dive
    Deeper into your inner version.

III. The channel inward remains
    Open before the next exploration.

XXXI — BRIDGING THE GAP

I.   The valley of accumulated thought
        Tempts to draw clarity
    From the present.

II.   Full unwavering attention
        Builds the high road.

III.   If all the ocean flows
        Under the bridge,
    The prior ocean forgives.

IV.   Bridging peaks of focus
        Reveals the inner version.

XXXII — VANISHING THREAT

I. Attaching to self-image,
   The threat identifies.

II. Comparing obstacles well-hurdled,
    The threat reframes.

III. With opportunity to grow,
     The threat disintegrates.

XXXIII — MODE INVERSION

I. Apprehension reverses
    Into eager anticipation.

II. Parallel thoughts rearrange
    Into sequential pleasure.

III. Problem-solving subsides
    Into perceptual freedom.

IV. Present-denial opens
    Into complete acceptance.

XXXIV — NO LOST EFFORT

I. Storm clouds pass through on occasion,
   Charging the senses transiently —
With such great opportunities
   Indebted to the present moment.

II. There is no lost effort
   On the trail to highest aspiration —
All paths arrive
   At your inner version.

XXXV — RESPONSE DELAY

I. Illusional urgency
 Tests the measured response.

II. Small steps back
 Compose giant strides.

XXXVI — CHANGING TIME FLOW

I. Frictionless travel
  Through differing intensity
 Improves response
  To the daily challenge.

II. From time to time, it can be beneficial
  To realign your inner version
 With the slow frequency
  Of the great unchanged.

III. Consciousness appears as many
  Speeds of thought —
  The faster is respected,
 The slower learns.

IV. The most natural state of being
  Occurs in the space
  Where time meanders
   And falls away.

XXXVII — THE WATCHER

I. The heron on the riverbank
    Silently watches the stream of thought,
    Choosing when to pursue
        Objects in the current —
    And when to return
To gentle observation.

II. The watcher notices
    In every thought,
    In every space
        Between every thought,
    And reunites
With your true inner version.

XXXVIII — COMFORT WITHIN

I. Catching silence
    Amidst the noise
Enlarges focus.

II. Finding comfort
    Within discomfort
Lowers the baseline.

XXXIX — OPPOSITE JOYS

I. Contemplation is delight
      In a thought;
    Meditation is delight
      In no thought.

II. Sense stimulation is joy
      In perception;
    Sensory silence is joy
      In anticipation.

XL — INFINITE JOY

I. Discovering new interpretations
　　Offers unbounded joy
To those applying wisely
　　Time and energy of mind.

II. With the realisation
　　Of a small but vital place,
Excitement arises
　　In a universe of infinite potential.

I –	PERSONAL PHILOSOPHY
II –	PONDER THE BEFORE
III –	ONE POINT
IV –	BECOMING LUCID
V –	SUSTAINING LUCIDITY
VI –	THE DREAM WORLD
VII –	THE SUBCONSCIOUS
VIII –	TWO STREAMS ALIGNED
IX –	BREAKING PATTERNS
X –	THE DELETE RULE
XI –	GROUNDED CREATION
XII –	THE WORK DIVERSE
XIII –	SWIRLS IN THE DUST
XIV –	THE DISCONNECT
XV –	ALMOST DESIRE
XVI –	PRESENT GREATNESS
XVII –	LOSS IN CONTROL
XVIII –	MODEST WISDOM
XIX –	MUTUAL REFLECTION
XX –	ENERGY FLOW

XXI –	OPEN TO THE WILD
XXII –	COMBINED RESET
XXIII –	ADVICE TWO WAYS
XXIV –	LIFE UNRATED
XXV –	HYPERBOLE AND OVER-HYPE
XXVI –	SIMPLE BEING
XXVII –	FIELD ALIGNMENT
XXVIII –	DAILY CONTRAST
XXIX –	SURFACE WAVES
XXX –	CHALLENGE THE DEEP
XXXI –	BRIDGING THE GAP
XXXII –	VANISHING THREAT
XXXIII –	MODE INVERSION
XXXIV –	NO LOST EFFORT
XXXV –	RESPONSE DELAY
XXXVI –	CHANGING TIME FLOW
XXXVII –	THE WATCHER
XXXVIII –	COMFORT WITHIN
XXXIX –	OPPOSITE JOYS
XL –	INFINITE JOY